Fat Quarter Quilts

M'LISS RAE HAWLEY

Martingale
& COMPANY

Bothell, Washington

CREDITS

President . . . . Nancy J. Martin
CEO/Publisher . . . . Daniel J. Martin
Associate Publisher . . . . .Jane Hamada
Editorial Director . . . . Mary V. Green
Design and Production Manager . . . . Cheryl Stevenson
Technical Editor . . . . .Ursula Reikes
Copy Editor . . . . .Tina Cook
Illustrator . . . . Laurel Strand
Photographer . . . . Brent Kane
Cover and Text Design . . . . Rohani Design

The Fat-Quarter Bag pattern on pages 70–72 is used
courtesy of Hancock Fabrics, Inc.

That Patchwork Place is an imprint of
Martingale & Company.

Fat Quarter Quilts
© 1999 by M'Liss Rae Hawley
Martingale & Company
PO Box 118
Bothell, WA 98041-0118 USA
www.patchwork.com

Printed in Canada
04 03 02 01   6 5

Library of Congress Cataloging-in-Publication Data

Hawley, M'Liss Rae,
      Fat quarter quilts / M'Liss Rae Hawley.
         p.   cm.
      ISBN 1-56477-269-1
      1. Patchwork Patterns.   2. Quilting Patterns.
I. Title.
      TT835.H346 1999
      746.46'041—dc21   99-25297
                                                  CIP

Patchwork is good economy. It is indeed a foolish waste of time to tear cloth into bits for the sake of rearranging it anew in fantastic figures; but a family may be kept out of idleness, and a few shilling saved, by thus using scraps of gowns, curtains, etc.

v Lydia Maria Child (1802–1880)
The American Frugal Housewife

DEDICATION

This book is dedicated to women and girls—and especially to teachers of sewing everywhere—who enjoy the feel of fabric, the beauty of textures, the precision of stitches, the smoothness of seams, and who delight always in appropriate fabrics carefully cut and made up for a happy purpose.

Mary Brooks Picken wrote the above dedication for *The Singer Sewing Book*, published in 1949. Mrs. Picken was a celebrity in her time.

She wrote ninety-two books and numerous magazine articles, and was featured on radio and television. She taught across the United States at schools and universities. Further, she founded and chaired many textile and fashion organizations still in existence today.

Although Mrs. Picken has become anonymous, fifty years later, people worldwide continue to stitch for love and glory. Here's to you all, especially the teachers of sewing everywhere.

ACKNOWLEDGMENTS

Living on Whidbey Island somewhat limits my access to fabric stores. I have two favorites: In The Beginning in Seattle, and Island Fabrics, etc., here in Freeland. I shop and teach at both of them.

Sharon E. Yenter, owner of In The Beginning, asked me to teach a class using six fat quarters. That class developed into this book. I am grateful for her guidance, kindness, and generosity. Her entire staff is helpful beyond belief, and Jason, Trish, Jackie, Gale, and Margy deserve special thanks. Thank you, Sharon!

Judy A. Martin, owner of Island Fabrics, etc., has been there through all the ups and downs. She provides me with fabulous fabric and friendship. Also the only Bernina dealer in Island County,

Judy makes certain all our Berninas keep stitching those perfect little stitches. Thank you, Judy!

Thank you to Keepsake Quilting in Centre Harbor, New Hampshire, which offers many wonderful fat quarter packets, some of which were used to make quilts for this book.

I'm also grateful to Tom Kelley and his daughter, Kathy Thompson, owners of Quilters Dream Cotton, Chesapeake, Virginia.

And thanks to my quilt group for helping with all these quilts!

Lastly, without Ursula Reikes, my editor, this book might not be. Thank you, Ursula, Kathryn Ezell, and all the staff at Martingale & Company. Although this is my second book, the process continues to be an incredible learning experience.

Contents

Introduction

They sit like open boxes of chocolate next to cash registers at quilt shops. They beckon us to touch them, to pick them up, and of course, to buy them! Hopelessly addicted, we stroll around the quilt shop noticing little packets neatly tucked into baskets, piled on shelves, and displayed with other trinkets. Just six 18" × 21" pieces of fabric—fat quarters—tied together with a pretty satin ribbon.

Mail-order catalogs entice us with fun little treats such as fat quarters rolled up in crayon boxes. Packets feature new fabric lines, holiday themes, seasonal collections, and juvenile prints. There are as many varieties of fat-quarter packets as there are quilters.

Working with fat-quarter packets is fast, fun, and easy:

➤ First, choose a quilt pattern.
➤ Second, buy your favorite packet of six fat quarters.
➤ Third, pick out a background fabric.
➤ And last, select one or more border fabrics.

For all the quilters who already have amazing stashes of fat quarters, do not despair. Your formula is altered only slightly. Choose six fabrics from your collection. (Don't panic, you can do it! Remember who purchased those fat quarters—you know you like them.) Begin with a color theme, a season, an event to commemorate, or just pick out six fabrics that you like. The rest of the formula is the same.

The quilts in this book range in size from a wall hanging to a large lap quilt. You can use the patterns to make a baby quilt, TV blanket, tablecloth, or picnic throw. If you want to enlarge a pattern, just add more fat quarters. For example, adding a second fat-quarter packet to Broken Bricks (page 47), plus additional background and border fabric, turns the lap quilt into a large twin quilt.

So, the next time your quilt group or guild has a fat-quarter party, you can attend with quilt and bag in hand for the ultimate in sharing. Warning: this is an addictive pattern of behavior. Proceed with caution!

General Directions

SUPPLIES

To make the projects in this book, you need the following supplies:

➤ 100% cotton fabric (a packet of six fat quarters, a background fabric, and one or more border fabrics)
➤ 100% cotton thread in a neutral color
➤ A sewing machine in good working order (A ¼" presser foot helps keep your piecing accurate—foot #37 on most Berninas.)
➤ ¼"-wide quilter's tape
➤ Fine, thin pins with glass heads
➤ Fabric scissors
➤ Seam ripper

In addition, you need the following rotary-cutting equipment:

➤ Rotary cutter
➤ Cutting mat
➤ 6" × 24" ruler
➤ Ruler grips. These adhesive tabs are available in plastic, sandpaper, and felt. Stick them to the bottom of your rulers to keep them from slipping while you cut.
➤ 4" Baby Bias Square® ruler for the Houndstooth quilt, 6" Bias Square ruler for the Roman Stripes quilt

FAT-QUARTER PACKETS

Technically, a fat quarter should measure 18" × 21". Practically, when you examine a packet of fat quarters, you may notice slight discrepancies in size. There are many possible reasons for this. While the industry standard for greige goods is 42" wide, some manufacturers' fabrics are slightly narrower. Also, the selvage and fabric identification take up some of the width, which means the fat quarter will be slightly shorter than 21" if the selvages were removed before the fat quarters were cut.

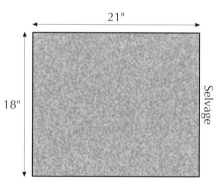

Another variable is the actual cut dimensions. While a perfectly cut fat quarter measures 18" × 21", some shops consistently cut theirs slightly smaller or larger.

I advocate prewashing (see "Preparing Your Fabric" on page 8), which will further alter the size of your fat quarters. Laundering often shrinks fabric slightly, and the washing machine can really fray small pieces of fabric.

Because of all the size variables, the patterns in this book are based on fat quarters that are 17" × 20" after prewashing. My advice is to measure all your fat quarters after you wash them. If your fat quarters are smaller than 17" × 20", you can easily add a seventh or eighth fabric to make up the difference.

On the other hand, your fat quarters may be bigger than 17" × 20". You can use the extra fabric to make more blocks, thereby making a larger quilt, or you can save the leftovers for another project.

You'll cut strips from the 20" length of the fat quarter for all patterns except Road to Ireland. For that pattern, you'll cut strips along the 17" width.

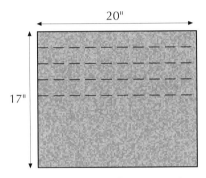

Cutting strips for most quilts

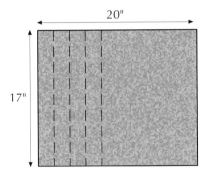

Cutting strips for Road to Ireland

Depending on the useable size of your fat quarters, you may be able to make more or fewer blocks than the directions call for. That's why, when you look at the photos in this book, you might see quilts made from the same pattern that are different sizes. The quilters made do with what they had.

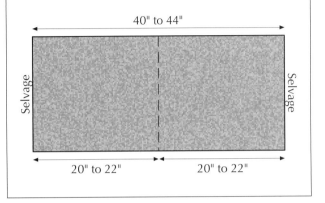

TIP: *If your local fabric store does not sell fat quarters, buy half-yard pieces. Cut the fabric along the fold to get two fat quarters! Trade with a friend, or stash one fat quarter for another quilt.*

CHOOSING THE RIGHT FABRIC

Fat-quarter packets are available in such tremendous variety that making choices can be overwhelming. I recommend that you pick the quilt pattern before you pick the fabric. It's easier to find the appropriate fat-quarter packet, background, and border fabric once you know what you intend to make.

"But Mom, I Still LOVE Red and Purple!" on page 24 was made from a one-color fat-quarter packet. The monochromatic fat quarters work in this quilt, but only because the texture of each red fabric is clearly different. A monochromatic color scheme may tempt you, but I've found that most of the designs in this book look best when made with a wide variety of colors printed with different patterns and textures.

Once you've chosen a fat-quarter packet, it's time to consider the background fabric. Should it be light or dark? A solid or a print? Look at the quilts on pages 17–46 and study the ones that appeal to you. What is the value and scale of the background fabrics? Also, consider the end use of your quilt. You might want a bright background for a baby quilt, a dark background for a tablecloth.

Your next step is the border. Most quilt shops make fat-quarter packets from newly arrived fabrics. This means the fabrics in the packet are usually still available on the bolt. Repeating one of the fat-quarter fabrics in the border is an easy and sure way to finish your quilt, as I did in my Roman Stripes quilt, "Our Whidbey Island Garden," on page 39. If the fabric you want is unavailable, consider one of the following options.

➤ Take the darkest color in the fat-quarter packet and go a little darker.
➤ If your fat quarters follow a theme—say, fairy prints—find a print that works thematically.
➤ If your packet includes a range of colors and patterns, select a floral or paisley print that ties them all together. See "Erin's Journey Home" on page 42 for an example.

The final step is the binding. Traditionally, the binding is the darkest fabric in the quilt or the same fabric as that used in the outer border. Now that you know this rule, you have permission to do whatever you want. I like to continue the theme of the outer border in the binding. For instance, if I used a floral print for the outer border, I use the same or another floral for the binding.

PREPARING YOUR FABRIC

When I bring fabric home, anything less than ½ yard goes into the bathroom. I wash it by hand with a liquid detergent (or more likely, my daughter, Adrienne, does!) and hang it to dry. Larger pieces go directly to the laundry room. I put them in the machine, run the water, and check to see if the colors run. If not, the rest of the load goes in and I continue the wash cycle. If the fabric bleeds, I keep rinsing it until the water runs clear.

I press all my fabric (actually, my husband and son do the pressing), then I square it up. If it is not a fat quarter, I cut off a 1½" strip. My plan is to someday make a Log Cabin quilt with my entire textile history.

ROTARY CUTTING

Rotary cutting is covered in many quilting books, some of which you probably already have on your shelf, so we won't go into detail here. The basic procedures are the same whether you're cutting fat quarters or full-length yardage. Before cutting strips from the fabric, you must first square up the edges.

Lay a fat quarter on your cutting mat. Place a 6" × 24" ruler perpendicular to the selvage. Use the selvage as your guide to square up the right-hand side. Turn the fat quarter around and square up the left-hand edge.

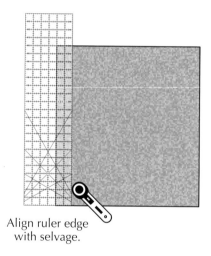

Align ruler edge with selvage.

Having established two straight edges, you are ready to begin cutting strips. Occasionally, your fat quarter will need to be squared up after two or three cuts. Repeat the squaring-up process, and resume cutting.

Houndstooth

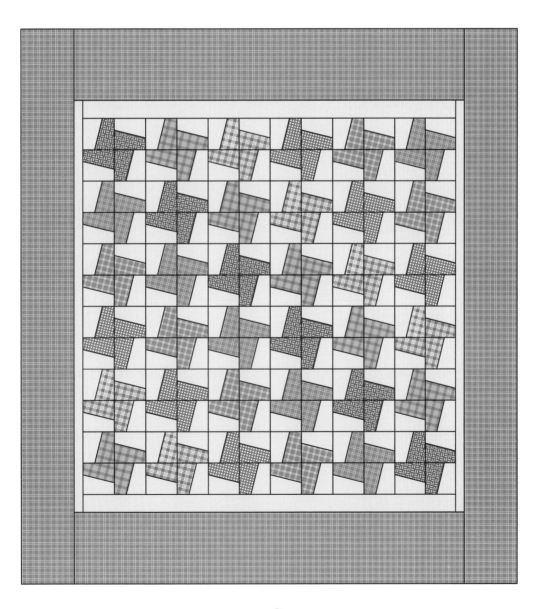

Finished Quilt 56" x 62"
Finished Block 7"

I was a weaver long before I was a quilter. Houndstooth has always been one of my favorite weaving patterns, so it seemed natural for me to adapt it for a quilt.

Although traditionally made in black and white, the Houndstooth pattern becomes even more interesting in color. Look at the quilts on pages 33–36 to see some fabric options.

MATERIALS: 42"-wide fabric

1 packet of 6 fat quarters
2 yds. for block background and inner border
1⅜ yds. for outer border
3½ yds. for backing
¾ yd. for binding
4" Baby Bias Square ruler
¼"-wide quilter's tape

CUTTING

Cut along the 20" length of the fat quarters.

From each fat quarter, cut:
  6 strips, each 2¾" × 20" (36 total)

From the background fabric, cut:
  18 strips, each 2¾" × 40"
  3 strips, each 1½" × 40", for inner side
    borders
  3 strips, each 2½" × 40"*, for inner top and
    bottom borders

From the outer border fabric, cut:
  3 strips, each 6½" × 40", for sides
  3 strips, each 8½" × 40", for top and bottom

From the binding fabric, cut:
  7 strips, each 3" × 40"

*If your fabric is 42½" wide after preshrinking, you need to cut only 2 strips.

DIRECTIONS

1. Sew 2 matching fat-quarter strips end to end to make 1 long strip. Press the seam to one side. Repeat with the remaining fat-quarter strips to make a total of 18 long strips.

Join.

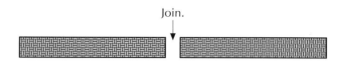

2. Sew a long fat-quarter strip to a 2¾"-wide background strip to make a strip unit. Press the seam toward the dark fabric. Repeat to make a total of 18 strip units.

3. Use the 4" Baby Bias Square ruler as a template to cut squares from the strip units. Lay the ruler on the Houndstooth template guide on page 12. Place a strip of ¼"-wide quilter's tape on the ruler, aligning it with the line on the guide. Draw arrows on the tape as shown. If you have ruler grips, place them on the bottom of the ruler at each corner to help keep the ruler in place while you cut.

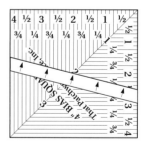

4. Starting at the right-hand end of a strip unit, place the edge of the tape on the seam line with the arrows pointing toward the seam. Trim the right-hand corner; discard the corner piece. Cut along the opposite edge of the ruler to separate the unit from the rest of the strip. Trim the remaining 2 edges of the square. Continue cutting squares in the same manner. Cut 8 squares from each strip unit for a total of 144.

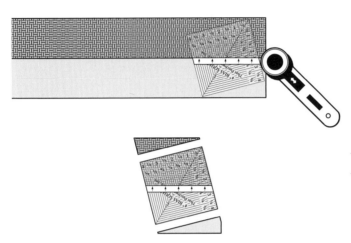

Note: If your strip units are at least 40" long, you will be able to cut 8 squares without including the seam in one of the squares. If your strip units are shorter, you may not be able to avoid the seam. Don't worry, the seam won't show when you join the squares.

> # TIP: *When cutting along the edges of the ruler, be careful to not twist the fabric. If you have a rotating cutting mat, use it when cutting the squares.*

5. Sew 4 matching units together to make each block. Caution: the block edges are on the bias, so handle them carefully. You can use spray starch or sizing to help keep the blocks stable. Stack matching blocks and label them 1–6.

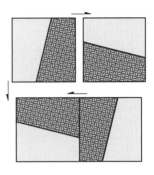

ASSEMBLY AND FINISHING

1. Arrange the blocks in 6 rows of 6 blocks each as shown. Rotate the blocks as needed so that the seams will nest together when sewn. Sew the blocks together in horizontal rows. Join the rows.

2. Staystitch around the quilt top, ⅛" from the raw edges. The edges are all on the bias, so handle them carefully.

3. Referring to "Adding Borders" on pages 73–74, sew the 2½"-wide inner border strips to the top and bottom edges of the quilt top, piecing as necessary. Sew the 1½"-wide strips to the sides.

4. For the outer border, repeat step 3, using 8½"-wide strips for the top and bottom edges and 6½"-wide strips for the sides.

5. Layer the quilt top with batting and backing; baste. Quilt as desired.

6. Bind the edges of your quilt. Add a label, and a sleeve pocket if desired.

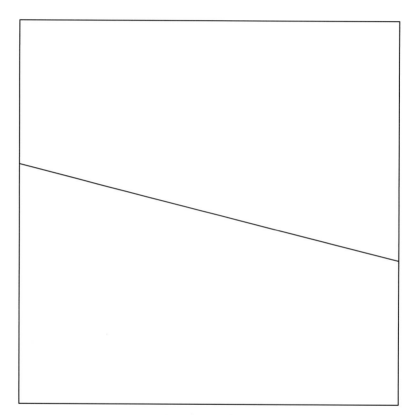

Houndstooth Template Guide

Roman Stripes

Finished Quilt 53½" × 58½"
Finished Block 5"

Roman Stripes is a traditional Amish quilt pattern that is usually made with dark, solid colors—some Amish communities even restrict the colors that may be included. Solid black is commonly used for the large half-square triangle.

Although solids may be traditional, you don't have to limit yourself to them. Prints of all varieties can be used throughout the quilt or in combination with solids.

When your blocks are complete, play with the layout before you piece the top. There are traditional settings you may want to use, or you may discover some new and wonderful settings of your own! Look at the quilts on pages 37–40 for inspiration.

MATERIALS: 42"-wide fabric

1 packet of 6 fat quarters
1 additional coordinating fat quarter
¼ yd. for inner border
1¼ yds. for outer border
1¼ yds. for background
3½ yds. for backing
⅝ yd. for binding
6" Bias Square Ruler

CUTTING

Cut along the 20" length of the fat quarters.

From each of the 6 fat quarters, cut:
    8 strips, each 1¾" × 20" (48 strips); keep
        the different strips in separate stacks

From the additional fat quarter, cut:
    6 strips, each 1¾" × 20"

From the inner border fabric, cut:
    5 strips, each 1¼" × 40"

From the outer border fabric, cut:
    6 strips, each 6½" × 40"

From the binding fabric, cut:
    6 strips, each 3" × 40"

DIRECTIONS

1. Sew 2 matching fat-quarter strips end to end to create 1 long strip. Press the seam to one side. Repeat to make 27 pieced strips. Joining strips increases the number of blocks you can cut.

2. Sew 3 different strips together to make a strip unit. Press the seams in one direction. See the sidebar at right for arrangement options.

TIP: *I establish which end of the strip unit is the top and stitch from that point down. It's less confusing when you consistently stitch all the strip units in the same direction.*

Arrangement Options

➤ Stitch together fabrics 1, 2, and 3; then 2, 3, and 4; then 3, 4, and 5. Sew together fabrics 4, 5, and 6; then 5, 6, and 7; then 6, 7, and 1; then 7, 1, and 2; then back to 1, 2, and 3. This format creates seven different color sequences. The last time through the stacks, you will be unable to continue the sequence. Just make sure that all three fabrics are different.

➤ Randomly pick up any three fabrics and stitch them together. A word of caution: select carefully as you approach the bottom of the stacks. Three different fabrics are required in each strip unit.

3. Measure the width of your strip units. If you stitched your strip units with perfect accuracy, they will measure 4¼" wide. If your strip units do measure 4¼" wide, cut 9 strips, each 4¼" × 40", from the background fabric.

If the strip units are not 4¼" wide, cut your background strips to match the width of your strip units. For example, if your strip units are only 4" wide, cut 4" × 40" background strips.

4¼"

4. With right sides together, place a strip unit on top of a background strip. Align the edges carefully and pin them together along both long sides. Stitch along both of the pinned edges. Repeat with the remaining strip units and background strips. Press the sets, using spray starch or sizing to help keep them flat.

5. Starting on the right-hand side of the unit, with the wrong side of the background strip facing you, place the 45° line of your ruler on the stitching line closest to you. Cut along the upper edge of the ruler. This first cut removes the corner.

6. Rotate the ruler and align the 45° line of the ruler with the opposite stitching line. Continue cutting the strip unit, rotating the ruler with every other cut. Cut 8 triangles from each strip unit, for a total of 72.

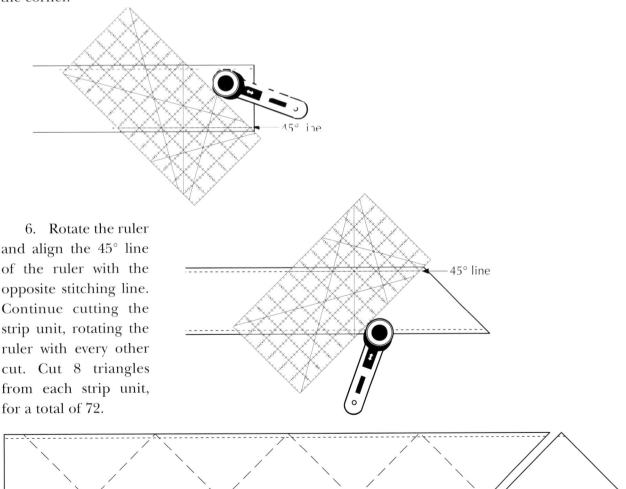

Cut 8 from each strip unit.

7. Use a seam ripper to remove the stitches at the point of each block. Gently lift the center point of the thread, and the seam will pull apart easily.

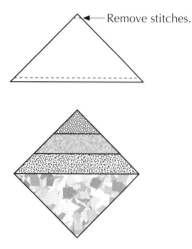

Remove stitches.

8. Working from the backs of the blocks, press the middle seam in the same direction as the seams in the strip units. Then press the front. Apply a little pressure at the seam line to give the block a crisp, clean look.

Note: These blocks have bias edges. Handle them gently and you won't have any problems.

9. Square up the blocks by placing the diagonal line of a Bias Square ruler on the center seam of the block. Trim the first 2 sides, then turn the block around and trim the other 2 sides. The blocks should measure 5½" after trimming.

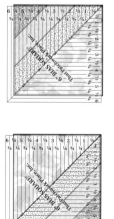

5½" line on edge of block

Note: If your seam allowances vary from the standard ¼", your blocks may be smaller or larger than 5½". If this is the case, you will need to measure the blocks to determine the smallest size, and then trim all the blocks to that size. If your blocks are only 5" after trimming, that's okay. The important thing to remember is that the blocks must all be the same size so they will fit together when you assemble the quilt top.

ASSEMBLY AND FINISHING

1. Referring to the quilt plan on page 13, arrange the blocks in 9 rows of 8 blocks each. Play with the layout before you join the blocks (you may want to look at Amish quilts to inspire you). Sew the blocks together in horizontal rows. Join the rows.

2. Press the quilt top from the back. Pressing from the back allows you to follow the direction of the seams, which will help keep the top as flat as possible. Turn the quilt top over and press again. Use spray starch or sizing if desired.

3. Because the edges of the quilt top are on the bias, it's a good idea to staystitch ⅛" from the raw edge all the way around the quilt. Stitch with the back facing up to make it easier to sew the seams in the correct direction.

4. Referring to "Adding Borders" on pages 73–74, sew the inner border to the top and bottom of the quilt top, then to the sides, piecing as necessary. Repeat for the outer border.

5. Layer the quilt top with batting and backing; baste. Quilt as desired.

6. Bind the edges of your quilt. Add a label, and a sleeve pocket if desired.

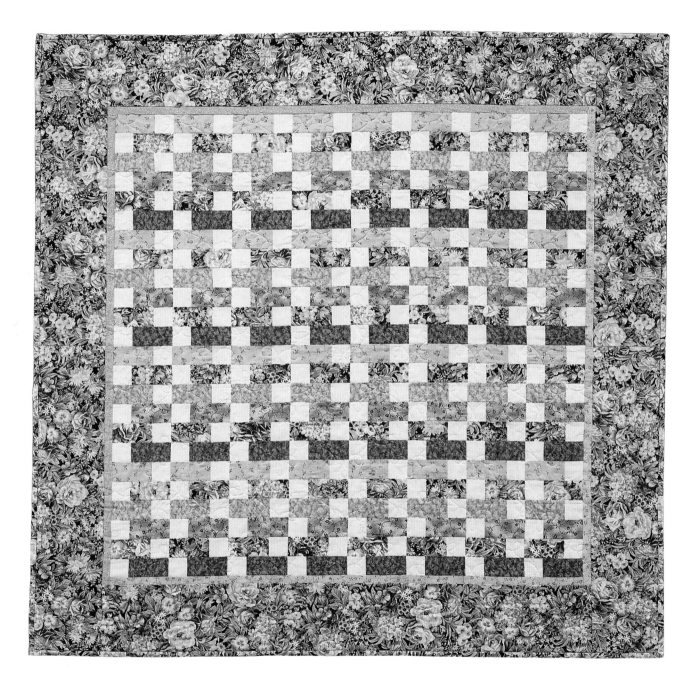

Broken Bricks: *Garden Party for Baby* by M'Liss Rae Hawley, 1998, Freeland, Washington, 57" × 55"; quilted by Doris Ellis.

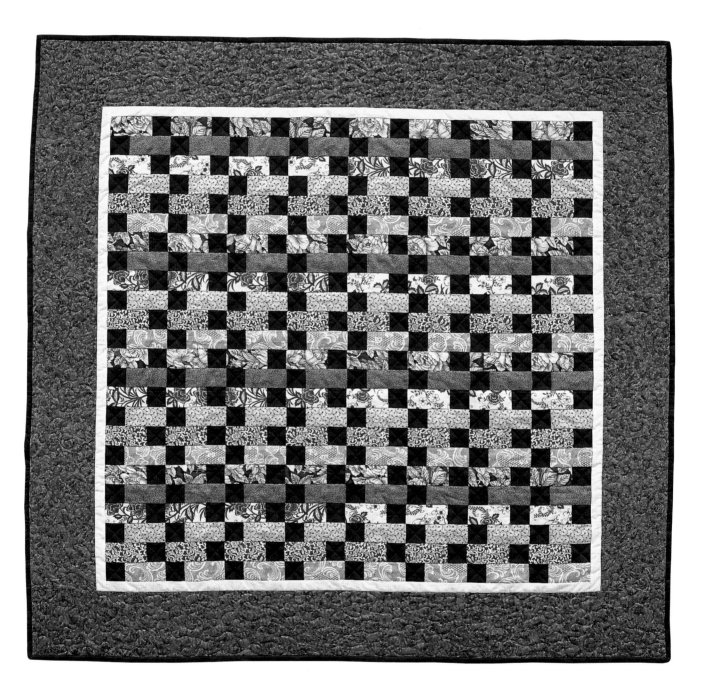

Broken Bricks: *Sew Blue Without You* by Linda Thomas, 1998, Everett, Washington, 58" × 55½".

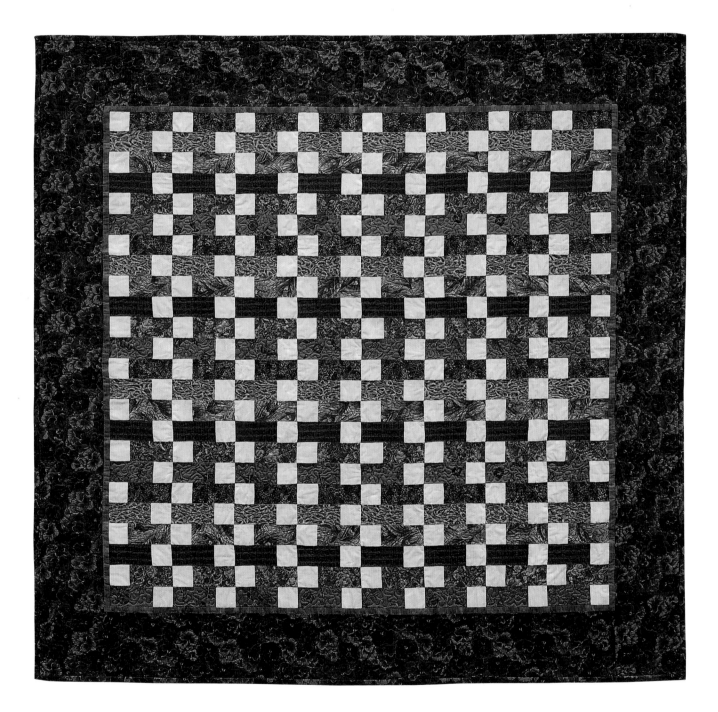

Broken Bricks: *Fields of Lavender* by M'Liss Rae Hawley, 1998, Freeland, Washington, 57" × 55"; quilted by Lorie Morrison.

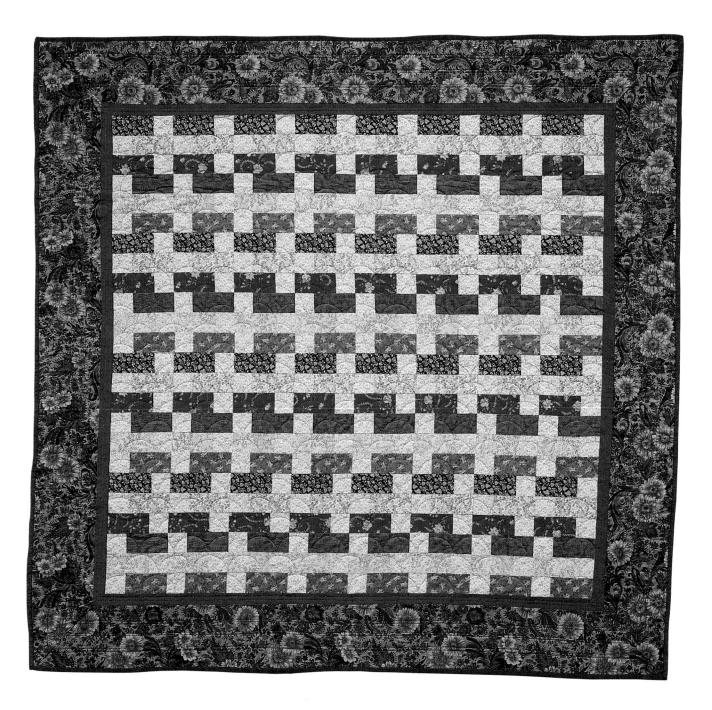

Broken Bricks: *Autumn Splendor* by Donna C. Lever, 1998, Maple Valley, Washington, 57" × 55"; quilted by Frankie Schmitt.

Fat Quarter Bag: *Fat Quarter Bag* by M'Liss Rae Hawley, 1998, Freeland, Washington.

Triangles and Confetti: *Easter Parade* by M'Liss Rae Hawley, 1998, Freeland, Washington, 48¼" × 63"; quilted by M'Liss Rae Hawley and Doris Ellis.

Triangles and Confetti: *Japanese Confetti* by M'Liss Rae Hawley, 1998, Freeland, Washington, 48¼" × 63"; quilted by M'Liss Rae Hawley and Doris Ellis.

Triangles and Confetti: *"But Mom, I Still LOVE Red and Purple!"* by M'Liss Rae Hawley, 1998, Freeland, Washington, 48¼" × 63"; quilted by M'Liss Rae Hawley and Doris Ellis.

Triangles and Confetti: *Flaming Batiks* by Christina Wright, 1998, Woodinville, Washington, 53" × 64".

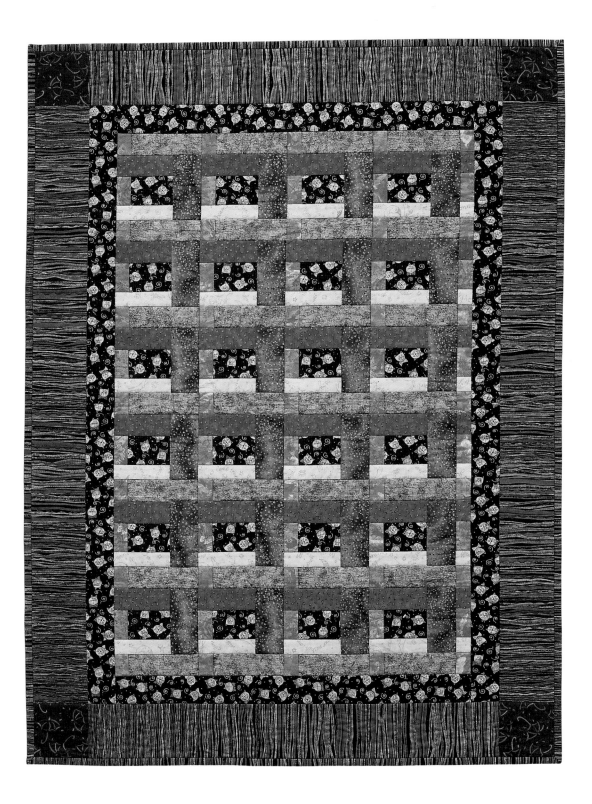

Woven Ribbons: *Molly's Kittens* by M'Liss Rae Hawley, 1998, Freeland, Washington, 37" × 50½".

Woven Ribbons: *My Early Morning Jolt* by Vicki DeGraaf, 1998, Langley, Washington, 37" × 50½".

Woven Ribbons: *Old Jewels* by Terry Martin, 1998, Snohomish, Washington, 37" × 55½".

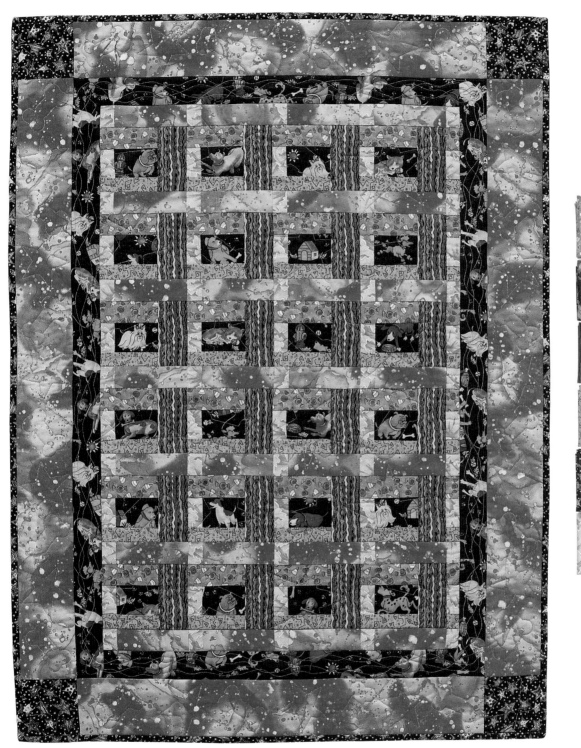

Woven Ribbons: *Third Fire Hydrant from the Sun* by Carol Atterberry, 1998, Monroe, Washington, 37" × 50½"; quilted by Maurine Noble.

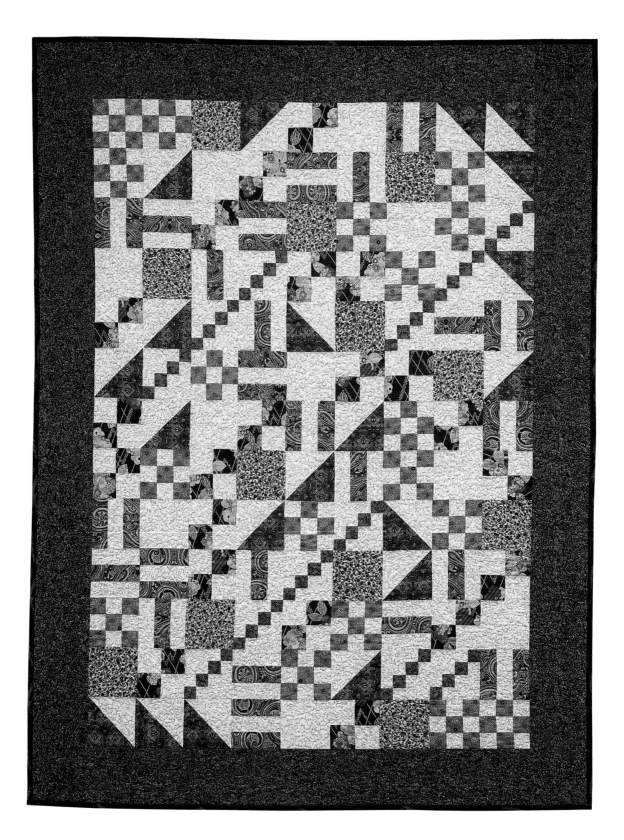

Mystery Sampler: *Mystery Solved* by M'Liss Rae Hawley, 1998, Freeland, Washington, 54½" × 68"; quilted by M'Liss Rae Hawley and Kris Desmarais.

Mystery Sampler: *Water Lily Medallion* by Tamara Petersen, 1998, Woodinville, Washington, 49" × 66".

Mystery Sampler: *Jed the Lone Star Roper* by Vicki DeGraaf, 1998, Langley, Washington, 56" × 65".

Houndstooth: *Dach's Hound's Tooth* by M'Liss Rae Hawley, 1998, Freeland, Washington, 56" × 62"; quilted by M'Liss Rae Hawley and Kris Desmarais.

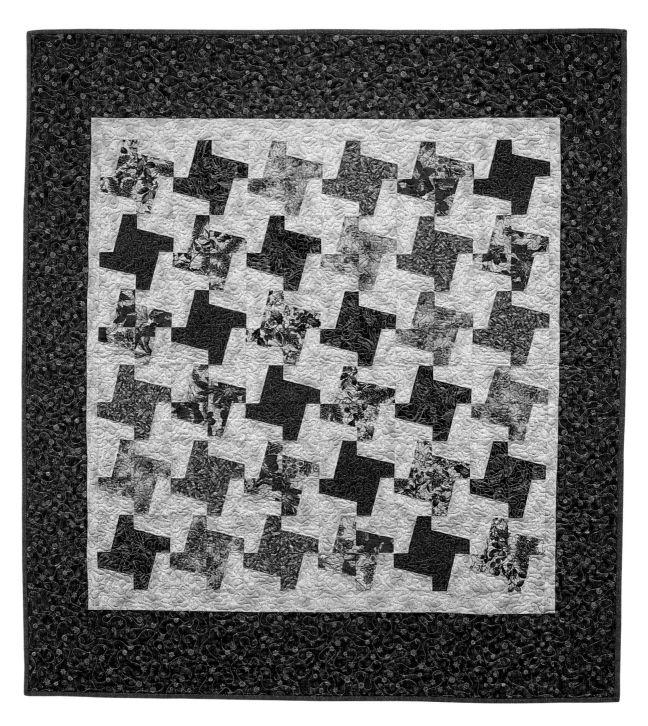

Houndstooth: *Sleigh Ride* by Beth Kovich, 1998, Woodinville, Washington, 54¾" × 60¾"; quilted by Frankie Schmitt.

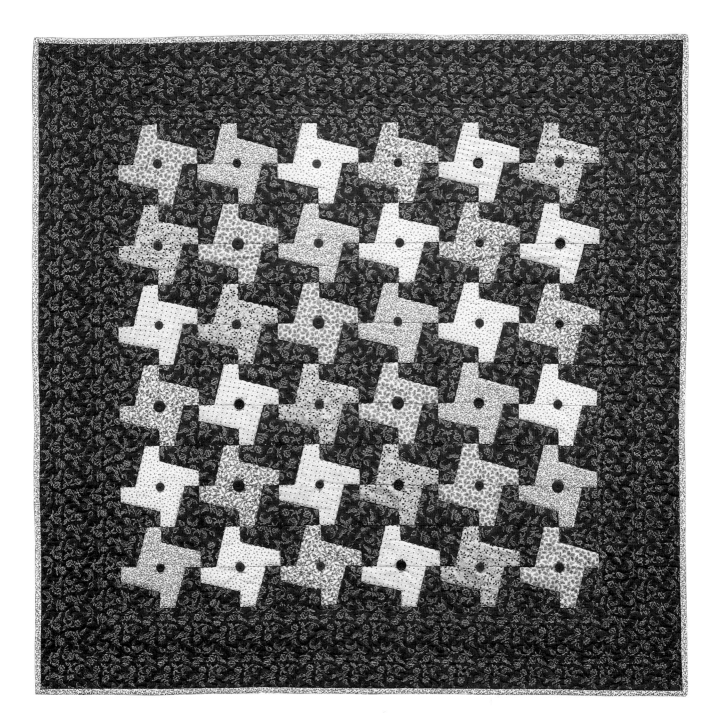

Houndstooth: *Montana Ruby* by Beth Kovich, 1998, Woodinville, Washington, 55¾" × 55¾"; quilted by Frankie Schmitt.

Houndstooth: *Asian Autumn* by M'Liss Rae Hawley, 1998, Freeland, Washington, 56" × 62"; quilted by Doris Ellis.

Roman Stripes: *Caesar Takes a Turkish Bath* by Julie Ketter, 1998, Everett, Washington, 51" × 56".

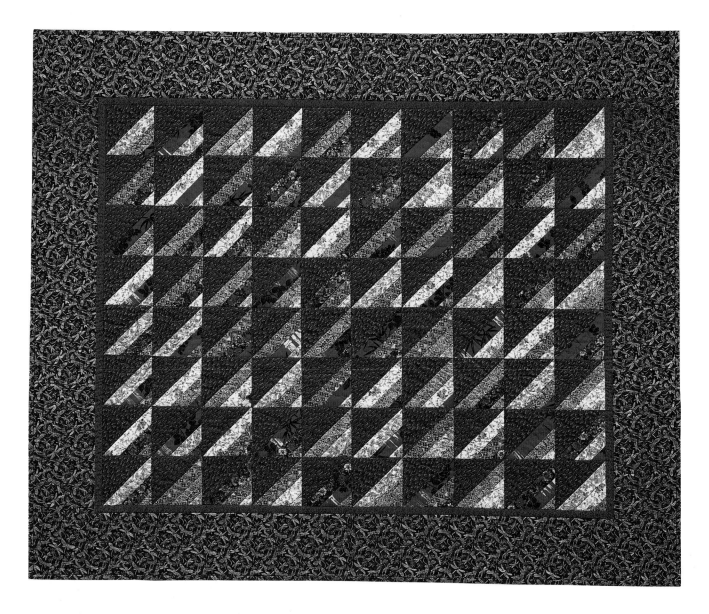

Roman Stripes: *Dragon Flies in the Garden* by Erin Rae Frandsen, 1998, Mukilteo, Washington, 53½" × 58½"; quilted by Barbara Dau.

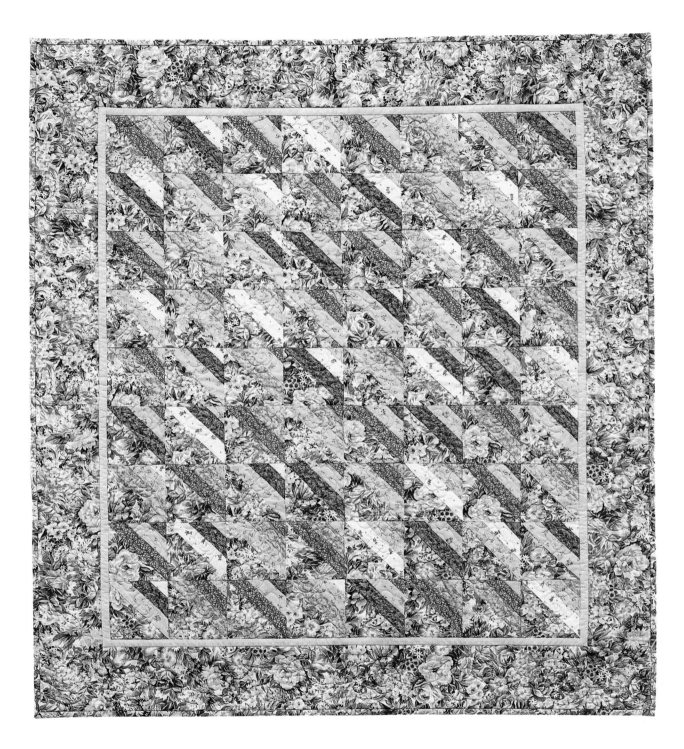

Roman Stripes: *Our Whidbey Island Garden* by M'Liss Rae Hawley, 1998, Freeland, Washington, 53½" × 58½"; quilted by Lorie Morrison.

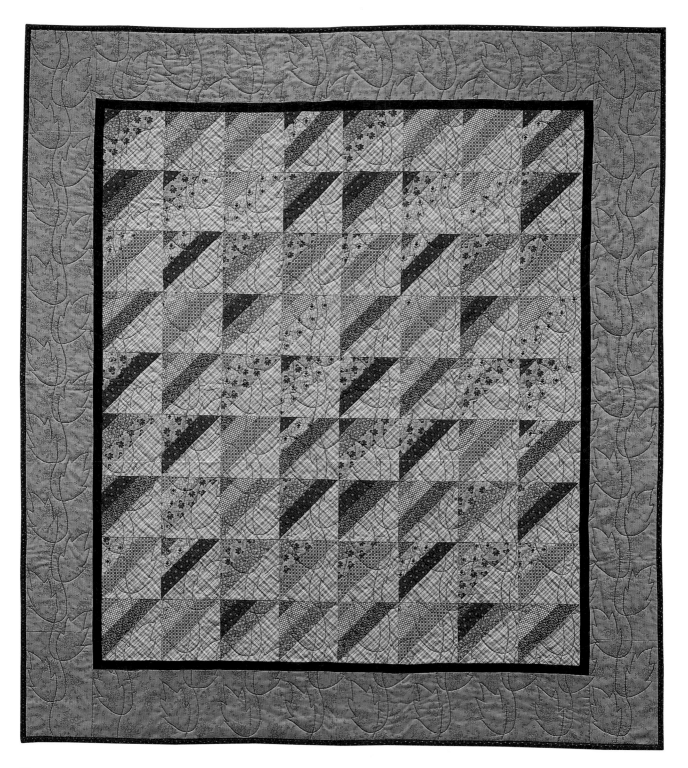

Roman Stripes: *Roman Plaid* by Carol DeGraaf, 1998, Kirkland, Washington, 53½" × 58½"; quilted by Kris Desmarais.

Road to Ireland: *Patti's Road to Ireland* by Rhoda A. Lonergan, 1998, Monroe, Washington, 34½" × 58".

Road to Ireland: *Erin's Journey Home* by M'Liss Rae Hawley, 1998, Freeland, Washington, 34½" × 58½".

Road to Ireland: *Sunset on the Road to Ireland* by Peggy Johnson, 1998, Langley, Washington, 42¼" × 54½"; quilted by Barbara Dau.

Skagit Fields: *A Day in Skagit Valley* by M'Liss Rae Hawley, 1998, Freeland, Washington, 51" × 58"; quilted by M'Liss Rae Hawley and Lorie Morrison.

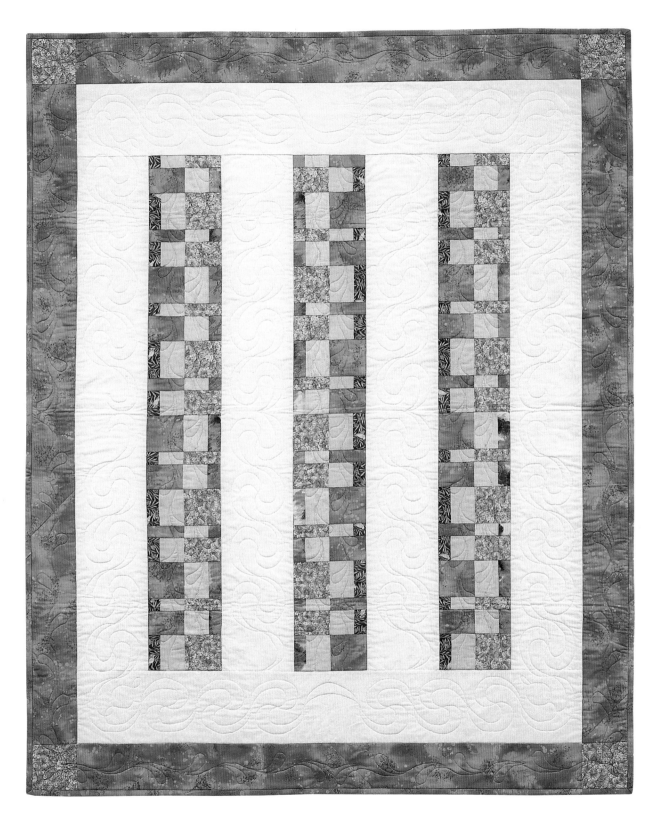

Skagit Fields: *My Spring Water Garden* by Peggy Johnson, 1998, Langley, Washington, 51" × 58"; quilted by Barbara Dau.

Skagit Fields: *Uncle Sam's Stars and Stripes* by Karen Mull Griffin, 1998, Seattle, Washington, 51" × 58"; quilted by Karen Mull Griffin and Lorie Morrison.

Broken Bricks

Finished Quilt 57" x 55"

When I decided to make a Brick-type quilt, I made several blocks and played with a variety of settings, but I could not find something that satisfied me. So I got out my graph paper, and the Broken Bricks pattern was born. Instead of blocks, there are rows of alternating brick and mortar sections. It turned out to be a simple and speedy quilt, one that could very easily be made larger. The real bonus, though, is the fun of making it. You are going to love it, and so will the person for whom you make it.

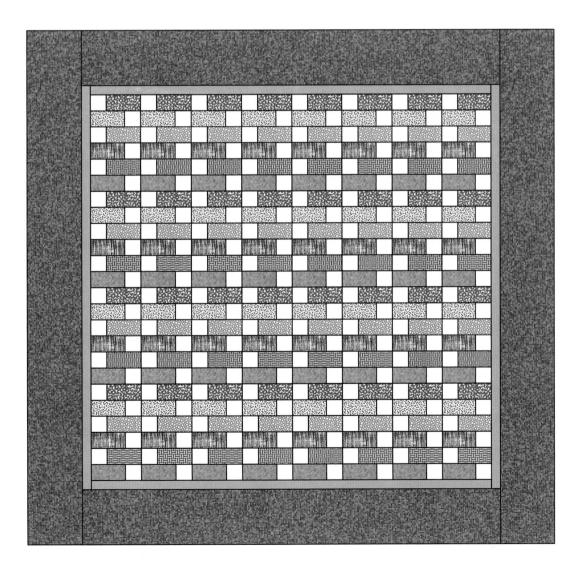

MATERIALS: 42"-wide fabric

1 packet of 6 fat quarters for bricks
⅞ yd. background fabric for mortar
¼ yd. for inner border
1¼ yds. for outer border
3½ yds. for backing
⅝ yd. for binding

CUTTING

Cut along the 20" length of the fat quarters.

From each of the 6 fat quarters, cut:
   4 strips, each 4¼" × 20", for bricks
      (24 total)

From the background (mortar) fabric, cut:
   12 strips, each 2¼" × 40". Cut the strips in
      half to make 24 strips, each 2¼" × 20".

From the inner border fabric, cut:
   5 strips, each 1½" × 40"

From the outer border fabric, cut:
   6 strips, each 6½" × 40"

From the binding fabric, cut:
   6 strips, each 3" × 40"

DIRECTIONS

1. Sew 4 matching fat-quarter strips and 4 mortar strips together as shown. Press the seam allowances toward the darker fabric. Repeat with the remaining brick and mortar strips. Cut 8 segments, each 2¼" wide, from each strip unit. You should have a total of 48 segments.

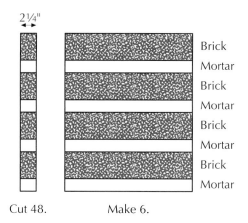

Cut 48.   Make 6.

2. Sew 2 matching segments end to end to make 1 long strip. Repeat with all the segments. You should end up with 24 long strips—4 long strips of each fat-quarter fabric. Stack matching long strips and label the stacks 1–6.

Join.

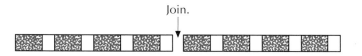

ASSEMBLY
AND FINISHING

1. Using 1 long strip from each stack, arrange the strips in numerical order, or in a color sequence of your choice. For the first row, use a strip that begins with mortar fabric. Turn the next strip around and start the second row with a brick fabric. Start the third row with a mortar fabric, the fourth row with brick fabric, and so on.

2. Sew the horizontal rows together 2 at a time: rows 1 and 2, 3 and 4, 5 and 6, and so on. Then join the pairs: 1–2 and 3–4, 5–6 and 7–8. Continue joining rows until all the rows are sewn together.

3. Referring to "Adding Borders" on pages 73–74, sew the inner border to the top and bottom edges of the quilt top, then to the sides, piecing as necessary. Press the seam allowances toward the border. Repeat for the outer border.

4. Layer the quilt top with batting and backing; baste. Quilt as desired.

5. Bind the edges of the quilt. Add a label, and a sleeve pocket if desired.

Row 1	Fabric #1
Row 2	Fabric #2
Row 3	Fabric #3
Row 4	Fabric #4
Row 5	Fabric #5
Row 6	Fabric #6
Row 1	Fabric #1
Row 2	Fabric #2
Row 3	Fabric #3
Row 4	Fabric #4
Row 5	Fabric #5
Row 6	Fabric #6
Row 1	Fabric #1
Row 2	Fabric #2
Row 3	Fabric #3
Row 4	Fabric #4
Row 5	Fabric #5
Row 6	Fabric #6
Row 1	Fabric #1
Row 2	Fabric #2
Row 3	Fabric #3
Row 4	Fabric #4
Row 5	Fabric #5
Row 6	Fabric #6

Mystery Sampler

Finished Quilt 54½" × 72½"

Finished Block 4½"

The Mystery Sampler blocks can be combined in an infinite number of arrangements. My Mystery Sampler, shown on page 30, is a perfect example of making use of what you have. The directions are based on fat quarters that measure 17" × 20" after prewashing; however, some of my laundered fat quarters measured 18" × 22", so I was able to make a few extra blocks. Play with what you have and make it truly your own.

MATERIALS: 42"-wide fabric

1 packet of 6 fat quarters
2 yds. for background
⅜ yd. for inner border (optional)
1¼ yds. for outer border
3½ yds. for backing
¾ yd. for binding

FABRIC SUGGESTIONS

Use a different fat quarter for each type of block. Assign and label the fat quarters before cutting. As you cut pieces for each block, store the pieces in individual zipper-lock bags.

Plain square: This is best suited for a focus fabric. Try a pictorial, a plaid, or even a bold geometric print.

Triple Rail: Use a medium- or dark-value print that will soften the columnar look. Avoid large-scale geometric prints.

Ocean Waves: Use a medium-value fabric, one that is not overpowering in color or scale.

Single Four Patch: This block shows an equal amount of background and fat-quarter fabric. Just about anything will work.

Double Four Patch: The darkest of your fat quarters will work best in this block, because only a small portion of the fat-quarter fabric will show.

Nine Patch: Almost any fabric works. For this block, I use whatever fat quarter is left over.

DIRECTIONS

Cut along the 20" length of the fat quarters.

Plain Squares

From fat quarter #1, cut:

    3 strips, each 5" × 20"; crosscut the strips into 12 squares, each 5" × 5"

Triple Rail

From fat quarter #2, cut:

    8 strips, each 2" × 20"

From the background fabric, cut:

    7 strips, each 2" × 20"

1. Sew the strips together to make 2 different strip units as shown. Press the seams toward the darker fabric.

2. Cut 12 squares, each 5" × 5", from strip unit 1, and 8 squares, each 5" × 5", from strip unit 2.

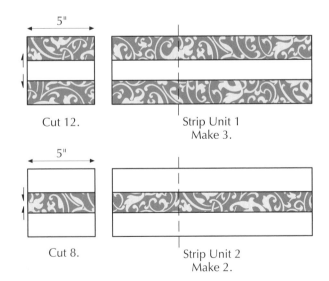

Cut 12.   Strip Unit 1 Make 3.

Cut 8.   Strip Unit 2 Make 2.

Ocean Waves

From fat quarter #3, cut:
   3 strips, each 5⅜" × 20"

From the background fabric, cut:
   3 strips, each 5⅜" × 20"

1.   Place a fat-quarter strip on top of a background strip, right sides together. Cut 3 squares, each 5⅜" × 5⅜", from the pair of strips. Cut the squares in half once diagonally. Repeat with the remaining strip pairs.

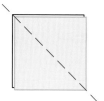

2.   Join triangle pairs along the long edges. Press the seam toward the darker fabric.

Make 18.

Four Patch

From fat quarter #4, cut:
   6 strips, each 2¾" × 20"

From the background fabric, cut:
   6 strips, each 2¾" × 20"

1.   Sew the fat-quarter and background strips together as shown. Press the seams toward the darker fabric. Cut 42 segments, each 2¾" wide, from the strip units.

2¾"

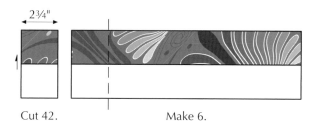

Cut 42.   Make 6.

2.   Stitch the segments together as shown. Press the seams toward one side.

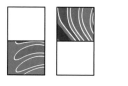

Make 21.

Double Four Patch

From fat quarter #5, cut:
   8 strips, each 1⅝" × 20"

From the background fabric, cut:
   8 strips, each 1⅝" × 20"
   4 strips, each 2¾" × 40"; crosscut the strips
      into a total of 48 squares, each 2¾" × 2¾"

1.   Sew the fat-quarter and background strips together as shown. Press the seams toward the darker fabric. Cut 12 segments, each 1⅝" wide, from each strip unit.

1⅝"

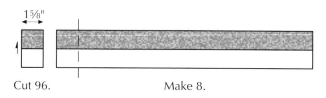

Cut 96.   Make 8.

2.   Join segments to make four-patch units.

Make 48.

3.   Join the four-patch units and the 2¾" squares as shown.

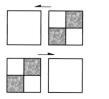

Make 24.

Nine Patch

From fat quarter #6, cut:
    8 strips, each 2" × 20"

From the background fabric, cut:
    7 strips, each 2" × 20"

1. Sew the fat-quarter and background strips together as shown to make 2 different strip units. Press the seams toward the darker fabric. Cut 25 segments, each 2" wide, from strip unit 1, and 20 segments, each 2" wide, from strip unit 2.

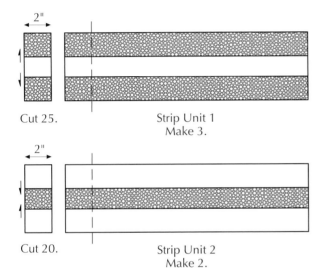

Cut 25. Strip Unit 1
Make 3.

Cut 20. Strip Unit 2
Make 2.

2. Arrange the segments as shown, then sew them together to make 2 sets of Nine Patch blocks.

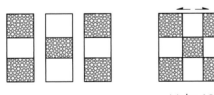

Make 10.

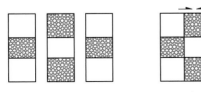

Make 5.

Additional Plain Squares

From the background fabric, cut 7 squares, each 5" × 5". If desired, cut additional squares to substitute for pieced squares.

Borders and Binding

From the inner border fabric, cut:
    5 strips, each 1½" × 40" (this border is optional)

From the outer border fabric, cut:
    6 strips, each 6½" × 40"

From the binding fabric, cut:
    7 strips, each 3" × 40"

ASSEMBLY AND FINISHING

1. Arrange the blocks, adding plain squares as necessary to create an interesting design. (Turn to pages 30–32 to see some great layouts for the Mystery Sampler.) Sew the blocks together in horizontal rows. Join the rows. Use any leftover blocks on the back of the quilt.

2. If you are adding an inner border, stitch the border to the top and bottom of the quilt, then to the sides, referring to "Adding Borders" on pages 73–74 and piecing as necessary. Repeat for the outer border.

3. Layer the quilt top with batting and backing; baste. Quilt as desired.

4. Bind the edges of the quilt. Add a label, and a sleeve pocket if desired.

Road to Ireland

Finished Quilt 35" x 59"

Finished Block 6"

One of my favorite fat-quarter quilts, Road to Ireland was a happy mistake. The blocks came out the way I had planned, but not the setting. (My planning consists of marks on napkins, ferry schedules, and the like.) So, I rearranged my blocks, and I love the result.

The Road to Ireland setting looks best when there is high contrast between the road fabric and the six fat quarters.

MATERIALS: 42"-wide fabric

1 packet of 6 fat quarters
½ yd. for "road" background
¼ yd. for inner border
⅞ yd. for outer border
1⅞ yds. for backing
½ yd. for binding

CUTTING

Cut strips from the fat quarters along the 17" length, parallel to the selvage.

Label the fat quarters 1–6. Assign numbers 1 and 6 to two of the strongest colors in your packet.

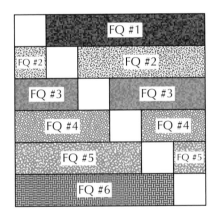

From fat quarter #1, cut:
   3 strips, each 5½" × 17"

From fat quarter #2, cut:
   3 strips, each 1½" × 17"
   3 strips, each 4½" × 17"

From fat quarter #3, cut:
   3 strips, each 2½" × 17"
   3 strips, each 3½" × 17"

From fat quarter #4, cut:
   3 strips, each 3½" × 17"
   3 strips, each 2½" × 17"

From fat quarter #5, cut:
   3 strips, each 4½" × 17"
   3 strips, each 1½" × 17"

From fat quarter #6, cut:
   3 strips, each 5½" × 17"

From the background fabric, cut:
   9 strips, each 1½" × 40"; cut the strips in
     half and trim to make 18 strips, each
     1½" × 17"

From the inner border fabric, cut:
   5 strips, each 1¼" × 40"

From the outer border fabric, cut:
   5 strips, each 5½" × 40"

From the binding fabric, cut:
   5 strips, each 3" × 40"

DIRECTIONS

1. Sew the fat-quarter and background strips together to make 6 different strip units as shown. Cut a total of 32 segments, each 1½" wide, from each strip unit.

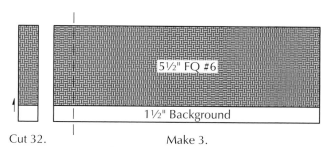

Cut 32.　　　　　Make 3.

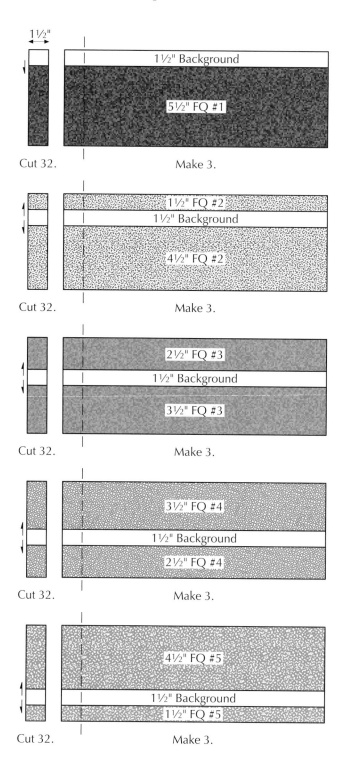

2. Arrange the segments as shown, then sew them together to make the blocks.

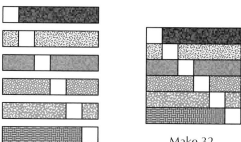

Make 32.

ASSEMBLY AND FINISHING

1. Referring to the quilt plan on page 54, arrange the blocks in 8 rows of 4 blocks each. Rotate the blocks as needed to form the "road."

2. Referring to "Adding Borders" on pages 73–74, sew the inner borders to the top and bottom of the quilt top, then to the sides, piecing as necessary. Repeat for the outer border.

3. Layer the quilt top with batting and backing; baste. Quilt as desired.

4. Bind the edges of your quilt. Add a label, and a sleeve pocket if desired.

Skagit Fields

Finished Quilt 51" × 58"

In early spring, acres of tulips and daffodils crisscross in rectangular patterns throughout the Skagit Valley. Skagit Fields is my interpretation of nature's glory. Whether you choose bright, funky prints or something more subdued, your quilt will be beautiful!

With only three widths—1½", 2½", and 3½"—the pieced bars are fast and fun to make. The large bars of background fabric are a perfect showcase for quilters. Skagit Fields is a nice size for a lap or baby quilt, and it also makes a great tablecloth.

MATERIALS: 42"-wide fabric

1 packet of 6 fat quarters
1⅜ yds. for background
⅞ yd. for border
3¼ yds. for backing
⅝ yd. for binding

CUTTING

Cut along the 20" length of the fat quarters.

From each of fat quarters #1 and #2, cut:
    4 strips, each 1½" × 20" (8 strips total)

From each of fat quarters #3 and #4, cut:
    4 strips, each 2½" × 20" (8 strips total)

From each of fat quarters #5 and #6, cut:
    4 strips, each 3½" × 20" (8 strips total)

From the lengthwise grain of the background, cut:*
    4 strips, each 6½" × 37½"
    2 strips, each 6½" × 42½"

From the leftover fat quarters, cut:
    4 squares, each 5" × 5", for corner squares

From the border fabric, cut:
    5 strips each, 5" × 40"

From the binding fabric, cut:
    6 strips, each 3" × 40"

*You might want to cut these strips after you've sewn the fat-quarter bars together, just in case your bars are shorter or longer.

DIRECTIONS

1. Sew the fat-quarter strips together to make 2 different strip units as shown.

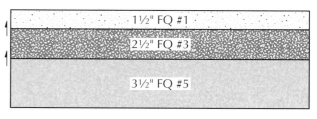

Strip Unit A
Make 4.

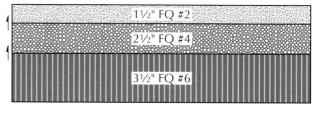

Strip Unit B
Make 4.

2. Cut segments from strip unit A as shown. Repeat with strip unit B.

3. Referring to the quilt plan on page 57, sew the pieced segments together in the following order.

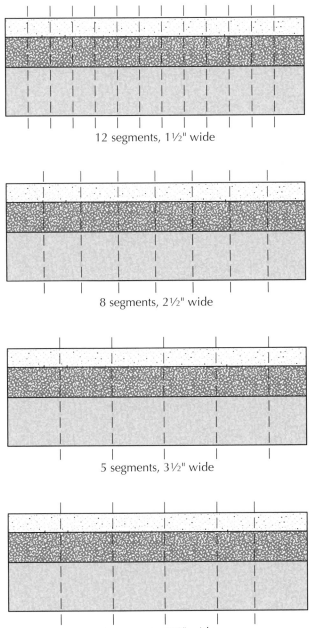

12 segments, 1½" wide

8 segments, 2½" wide

5 segments, 3½" wide

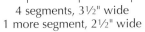

4 segments, 3½" wide
1 more segment, 2½" wide

MAKE 2 BARS	MAKE 1 BAR
1. (A) 1½" × 6½"	1. (B) 1½" × 6½"
2. (B) 2½" × 6½"	2. (A) 2½" × 6½"
3. (A) 3½" × 6½"	3. (B) 3½" × 6½"
4. (B) 1½" × 6½"	4. (A) 1½" × 6½"
5. (A) 2½" × 6½"	5. (B) 2½" × 6½"
6. (B) 3½" × 6½"	6. (A) 3½" × 6½"
7. (A) 1½" × 6½"	7. (B) 1½" × 6½"
8. (B) 2½" × 6½"	8. (A) 2½" × 6½"
9. (A) 3½" × 6½"	9. (B) 3½" × 6½"
10. (B) 1½" × 6½"	10. (A) 1½" × 6½"
11. (A) 2½" × 6½"	11. (B) 2½" × 6½"
12. (B) 3½" × 6½"	12. (A) 3½" × 6½"
13. (A) 1½" × 6½"	13. (B) 1½" × 6½"
14. (B) 2½" × 6½"	14. (A) 2½" × 6½"
15. (A) 3½" × 6½"	15. (B) 3½" × 6½"
16. (B) 1½" × 6½"	16. (A) 1½" × 6½"
17. (A) 2½" × 6½"	17. (B) 2½" × 6½"
18. (B) 3½" × 6½"	18. (A) 3½" × 6½"
19. (A) 1½" × 6½"	19. (B) 1½" × 6½"

ASSEMBLY AND FINISHING

1. Arrange the bars and 37½" background strips as shown below, then sew them together. Press the seams toward the background strips.

2. Stitch the remaining background strips to the top and bottom edges of the quilt top. Press the seams toward the background strips.

3. Referring to "Adding Borders" on pages 73–74, sew the border strips to the top and bottom edges of the quilt top, piecing as necessary. Press the seams toward the border.

4. Measure your quilt top through the center to determine its length. Trim the remaining borders to match the measurement, then add a corner square to each end. Stitch the borders to the sides of the quilt top, piecing as necessary. Press the seams toward the border.

5. Layer the quilt top with batting and backing; baste. Quilt as desired.

6. Bind the edges of your quilt. Add a label, and a sleeve pocket if desired.

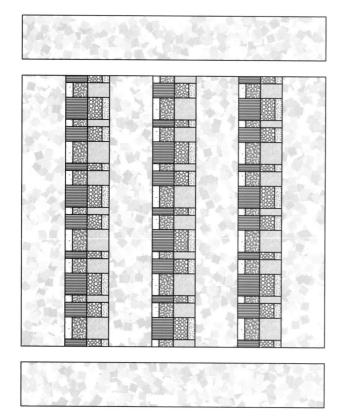

Triangles and Confetti

Finished Quilt 48¼" × 63"

Most quilters want to make a triangle quilt at some point, and there are several different cutting and piecing methods. After attempting most of them, I came up with the following technique for cutting the equilateral triangles. It doesn't require a template, nor does it demand fancy turns or cutting.

This project takes a little more time to make than some of the other quilts in this book, but it is well worth the effort.

MATERIALS: 42"-wide fabric

1 packet of 6 fat quarters
1 additional coordinating fat quarter
2½ yds. for background and border
3⅛ yds. for backing
⅝ yd. for binding

CUTTING

Cut along the 20" length of the fat quarters.

From each fat quarter, cut:
   4 strips, each 4" × 20" (28 strips total).
      Stack each fabric separately, right side
      up. Reserve the remaining fabric for
      confetti triangles in the border.

From the background fabric, cut:
   13 strips, each 4" × 40", for triangles
   5 strips, each 6½" × 40", for border

From the binding fabric, cut:
   6 strips, each 3" × 40"

CUTTING
THE TRIANGLES

1. Work with 1 stack of fat-quarter strips at a time, right sides up. Place the 60° line of a ruler on the edge closest to you. Cut along the upper edge of the ruler. This first cut removes the corner.

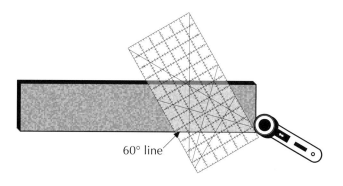

60° line

2. Turn the stack around so the cut edge is on the left. Place the 4" line of the ruler on the newly cut edge, and the 60° line on the bottom edge. Cut along the right side of the ruler to cut your first parallelogram. Cut 2 more parallelograms from the strip. The lower right corner of the fourth segment will be missing. Don't worry about this; you'll cut 1 triangle from this piece instead of 2.

Continue cutting parallelograms from the remaining strips. If your fat quarters are at least 21" long, you'll be able to cut 4 complete parallelograms from each strip. Save the excess fabric for the confetti triangles in the border.

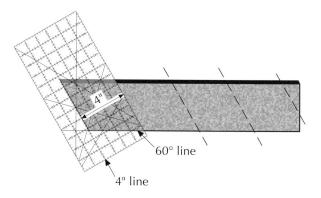

4"

60° line

4" line

> **TIP:** *If you have a 4"-wide rotary ruler, use it. It will make cutting all those parallelograms foolproof.*

3. Lay a ruler across a stack of parallelograms as shown and cut from corner to corner to get 2 sets of equilateral triangles. You'll get only 1 triangle from the fourth segment. Repeat with all the parallelograms to cut a total of 196 triangles.

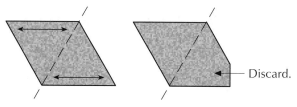

Discard.

Fourth segment

Note the position of the straight grain in each parallelogram, indicated by arrows in the previous illustration. As you cut, turn the first triangle so the straight grain is at the bottom, and stack it on top of the second triangle. Repeat with all the triangles, keeping matching triangles in 1 stack with the straight grain always on the bottom.

5. Repeat steps 1–4 with the 4"-wide background strips, cutting 8 parallelograms from each strip. Cut the parallelograms into a total of 195 triangles. Divide the background triangles into 6 stacks of 28 triangles and 1 stack of 27 triangles, each with the straight grain at the top.

Note: If the eighth segment has a clipped corner, you'll still be able to cut enough triangles for the quilt.

PIECING THE ROWS

Sew the triangles together to make 8 odd-numbered rows and 8 even-numbered rows as shown below. Odd-numbered rows start and end with a fat-quarter triangle. Even-numbered rows start and end with a background triangle. If you follow the pressing directions, the seams will nest perfectly when you join the rows.

Note: You can sew the fat-quarter triangles to background triangles randomly or you can follow a sequence. I labeled my fat-quarter stacks 1–7 and started the first row with fat-quarter #1, the second row with fat-quarter #2, the third row with fat-quarter #3, and so on through #7. I then started the sequence again with fat-quarter #1. Sewing in sequence creates diagonal lines of matching fat-quarter triangles.

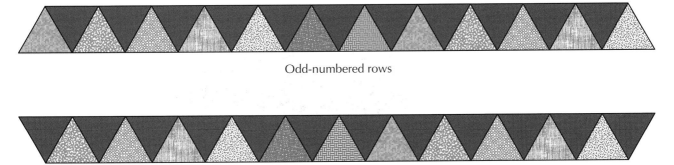

Odd-numbered rows

Even-numbered rows

1. Lay the 7 stacks of fat-quarter triangles in their color sequence (if you're using one) to the left of your machine, with the straight grain at the bottom. Place the stacks of background triangles between each fat-quarter stack, with the straight grain at the top.

FQ #1 FQ #2 FQ #3 FQ #4 FQ #5 FQ #6 FQ #7

2. Start the first row (an odd-numbered row) by sewing a fat-quarter #1 triangle to a background triangle. Sew a fat-quarter #2 triangle to a background triangle. Repeat with fat-quarter triangles #3–#7. Then, starting again with fat-quarter #1, sew fat-quarter triangles to background triangles to make 11 pairs. Press the seams toward the fat-quarter triangles.

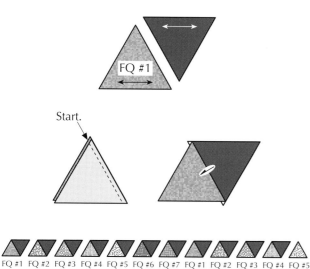

3. Sew the triangle pairs together. Press the seam toward the background triangle, *not* the fat-quarter triangle. End the row with a fat-quarter #5 triangle.

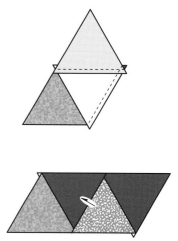

4. Begin row 2 (an even-numbered row) by sewing a background triangle and a fat-quarter #2 triangle together as shown. Press the seam toward the fat-quarter triangle. Sew the next background triangle to a fat-quarter #3 triangle. Continue sewing background and fat-quarter triangles in pairs to make 11 pairs. Join the pairs, pressing the seams toward the background triangles. End the row with a background triangle. Press the seams toward the background triangles when joining the pairs.

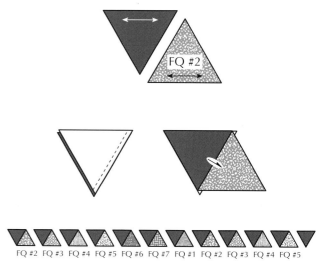

5. Continue sewing triangles together to make 16 rows. Remember, odd-numbered rows start and end with a fat-quarter triangle, and even-numbered rows start and end with a background triangle. You can use the leftover triangles in the border.

ASSEMBLY AND FINISHING

1. Sew the rows together in pairs: 1 and 2, 3 and 4, and so on. Then sew the pairs together. If you placed the straight grain in the triangles properly, you will be sewing on the straight grain across the row. Place a pin through each point, then insert another just to the right of the point. Stop and remove the pins as you stitch across the row.

2. Press the quilt top from the wrong side, following the seams as best you can. Then press from the front. Use spray starch or sizing if desired.

3. Square up the sides of the quilt top. Place the ¼" line of the ruler at the point where 2 triangles meet. Use a rotary cutter to trim the excess.

4. Since the sides of the quilt are on the bias, staystitch ⅛" from the raw edges. Stitch with the back facing up to make it easier to sew the seams in the correct direction.

5. Referring to "Adding Borders" on pages 73–74, sew the border to the top and bottom of the quilt top, then to the sides, piecing as necessary. Press the seams toward the border.

6. Cut triangles for the confetti border from the leftover fat quarters. The size of the triangles is up to you. If your leftover strips are narrower than 1½", that's okay. Just make small triangles. Cut the triangles following steps 1–3 on page 62.

7. Place the confetti triangles on the border randomly. Hold them in place with fusible web or fabric glue. Stay within ¾" of the outer edge. You can also use fabric spray adhesive (I like Sulky KK 2000) to temporarily baste the triangles in place. But you must do this after quilting the background triangles. Otherwise, the triangles will fall off while you're quilting.

8. Layer the quilt top with batting and backing; baste. Stipple quilt the background triangles. Stipple quilt the border, making certain to catch the corners of the triangles as you stitch.

9. Bind the edges of your quilt. Add a label, and a sleeve pocket if desired.

¼" seam allowance

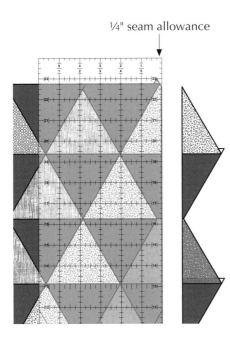

Woven Ribbons

Finished Quilt 37" x 50½"
Finished Block 6"

Woven Ribbons is a fun little quilt to make, and a great chance to take advantage of a favorite theme fabric. In my quilt on page 26, I used a whimsical cat fabric for the center of the blocks and for the inner border. I used five fat-quarter fabrics in the blocks, and reserved the sixth for corner squares in the outer border.

This quilt is the perfect size for a baby quilt or wall hanging. Once you've chosen the fabric placement and cut all the strips, it goes together quickly.

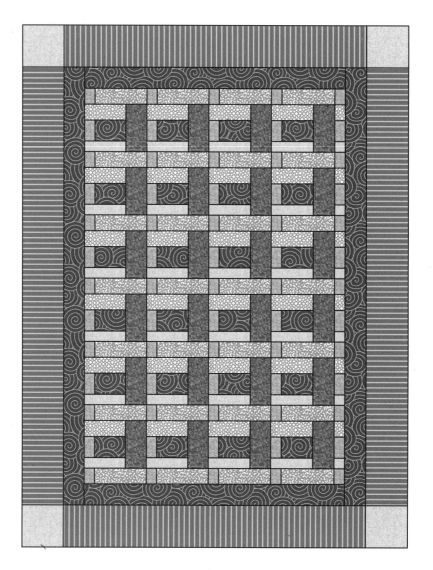

MATERIALS: 42"-wide fabric

1 packet of 6 fat quarters

¾ yd. background fabric for block centers and inner border*

¾ yd. for outer border

1⅝ yds. for backing

½ yd. for binding

*If you want to fussy-cut the block centers, you will need additional yardage.

CUTTING

Number the fat quarters from 1–5, to correspond with the block diagram. Use fat quarter #6 for the corner squares in the outer border. Cut along the 20" length of the fat quarters.

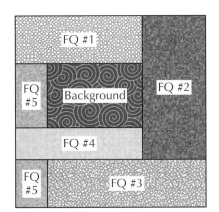

From fat quarter #1, cut:
    6 strips, each 2" × 20"
    1 strip, 2" × 12"

From fat quarter #2, cut:
    6 strips, each 2½" × 20"

From fat quarter #3, cut:
    3 strips, each 5½" × 20"

From fat quarter #4, cut:
    6 strips, each 1½" × 20"
    1 strip, 1½" × 12"

From fat quarter #5, cut:
    6 strips, each 1½" × 20"
    1 strip, 2½" × 12"
    1 strip, 2" × 12"
    1 rectangle, 1½" × 2"

From fat quarter #6, cut:
    4 squares, each 4½" × 4½", for corner squares

From the background fabric, cut:
    3 strips, each 3½" × 20", for block centers
    5 strips, each 2½" × 40", for inner border*

From the outer border fabric, cut:
    5 strips, each 4½" × 40"

From the binding fabric, cut:
    5 strips, each 3" × 40"

*If your fabric is at least 42" wide after preshrinking, you need to cut only 4 strips for the inner border.

DIRECTIONS

1. Sew 20"-long fat-quarter #5 and background strips together as shown to make strip unit 1. Cut 24 segments, each 2½" wide, from the strip unit.

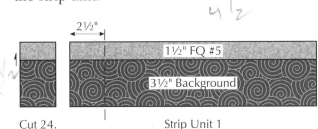

2½"

1½" FQ #5

3½" Background

Cut 24.

Strip Unit 1
Make 3.

2. Sew 20"-long fat-quarter #3 and fat-quarter #5 strips together as shown to make strip unit 2. Cut 28 segments, each 2" wide, from the strip unit (set aside 4 segments for the top row).

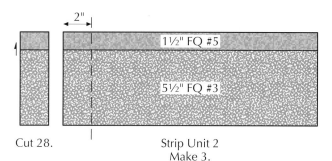

2"

1½" FQ #5

5½" FQ #3

Cut 28.

Strip Unit 2
Make 3.

3. Sew 12"-long fat-quarter #1, #4, and #5 strips together as shown to make a strip unit for the right inner border. Cut 6 segments, each 1½" wide.

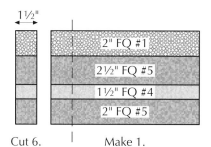

1½"

2" FQ #1

2½" FQ #5

1½" FQ #4

2" FQ #5

Cut 6.

Make 1.

4. Place the segments from strip unit 1 on top of a 20"-long fat-quarter #1 strip, right sides together and fat-quarter #5 closest to you. Position segments next to each other without overlapping the edges. Stitch. Cut between the segments, trimming any excess fabric. Press the seam allowance toward fat-quarter #1. Repeat with the remaining segments and fat-quarter #1 strips.

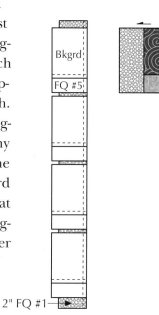

Bkgrd

FQ #5

2" FQ #1

5. Place the units from step 4 on top of a 20"-long fat-quarter #4 strip, right sides together and the background piece closest to you. Sew the units to the strip as in the previous step. Press the seam toward fat-quarter #4. Repeat with the remaining units and fat-quarter #4 strips.

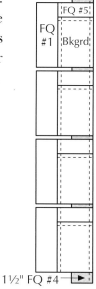

FQ #5

FQ #1

Bkgrd

1½" FQ #4

6. Place the units from step 5 on top of a fat-quarter #2 strip, right sides together and fat-quarter #1 closest to you. Sew the units to the strip as in the previous steps. Press the seam toward fat-quarter #2. Repeat with the remaining units and fat-quarter #2 strips.

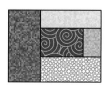

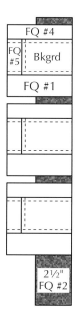

FQ #4

FQ #5

Bkgrd

FQ #1

2½" FQ #2

7. Sew the fat-quarter #3/#5 segments from step 2 to the bottom of the units to complete the blocks.

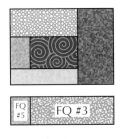

Make 24.

ASSEMBLY AND FINISHING

1. Referring to the quilt plan on page 66, arrange the blocks in 6 rows of 4 blocks each. Sew the blocks together in horizontal rows. Join the rows.

2. Sew the remaining fat-quarter #3/#5 segments end to end. Stitch to the top of the quilt.

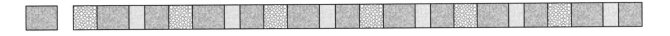

3. Sew the fat-quarter #1/#4/#5 segments together end to end to make the side row. Sew the 1½" × 2" fat-quarter #5 rectangle to the left end. Stitch to the right-hand side of the quilt top, placing the fat-quarter #5 rectangle at the top.

4. Referring to "Adding Borders" on pages 73–74, sew the inner border to the top and bottom edges of the quilt, then to the sides, piecing as necessary. Press the seams toward the border. Repeat for the outer border.

5. Layer the quilt top with batting and backing; baste. Quilt as desired.

6. Bind the edges of your quilt. Add a label, and a sleeve pocket if desired.

Fat-Quarter Bag

The Fat-Quarter Bag is a fast and fun project. It goes together so quickly you'll want to make one for everyone on your gift list. The bag holds a lot of quilt projects and is a good size for a child's overnighter.

MATERIALS: 42"-wide fabric

1 packet of 6 fat quarters
2⅛ yds. for lining and handles
¼ yd. flannel for handles
22" of 1"-wide non-roll elastic

CUTTING

From each of the six fat quarters, cut:
    1 rectangle, 17½" × 19½" (6 total)

From the lining fabric, cut:
    1 rectangle, 38½" × 51½", for lining
    4 strips, each 2½" × 40", for handles*

From the flannel, cut:
    2 strips, each 2½" × 40"**

*For longer handles, cut 8 strips.
**For longer handles, cut 4 strips.

DIRECTIONS

1. Arrange the 6 fat-quarter pieces as shown. Stitch or serge the pieces together. Press the seams to one side.

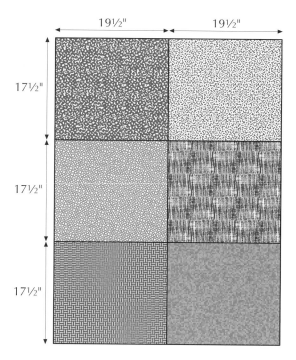

2. Pin the lining and the joined fat quarters right sides together. Using a ¼"-wide seam allowance, stitch or serge around the edges. Leave an 8" opening near the center at one short end. Turn the bag right side out.

3. To make the handles, place 2 lining strips right sides together and place a strip of flannel on top. Stitch or serge around 3 sides, leaving 1 short end open for turning. Turn the handle right sides out. Slipstitch the end of the handle closed. Topstitch ¼" from the edge all around both handles.

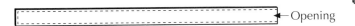

Note: To make longer handles, join 2 strips of fabric end to end to make 1 long strip. Make 4 long strips. Repeat with pairs of flannel strips. Follow the directions in step 3 to make the handles.

4. Press around the edge of the bag. Topstitch along the edge, beginning at the opening and ending at the other side of the opening. Do not stitch across the opening.

TIP: *It helps to pin the pressed edges before you topstitch. The pins hold the layers firmly in place as you sew.*

5. To make casings for the elastic, measure 7" from the short ends of the bag on both long edges and mark. Stitch from point to point, 1¼" from the topstitching.

6. Cut the elastic in half to yield 2 pieces, each 11" long. Working through the 8" opening, insert the elastic into both casings. Pin securely at both ends. Secure the ends of the elastic by stitching an ✕ in a 1" square.

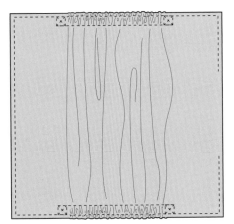

7. Slipstitch the open end of the bag closed. Continue topstitching across the 8" span.

8. To make the casing for the handles, fold 2" of both short ends toward the lining. Topstitch along the existing topstitching and ¼" from the fold.

9. Insert a handle into each casing. Holding handle pairs together, tie the ends in a knot.

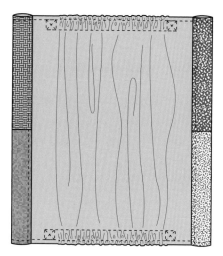

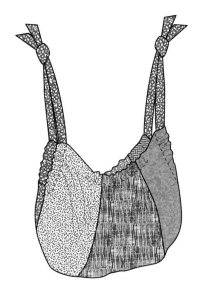

Quilt Finishing

ADDING BORDERS

The quilts in this book feature borders with straight-cut corners and borders with corner squares. Most of the instructions call for the border strips to be cut across the width of the fabric. The yardage requirements call for the minimum number of strips that will fit around the quilt top, which means that some of the borders need to be pieced. To piece border strips, sew them together end to end, then trim to the required lengths. If you prefer to center the seam of a pieced border at the edge of the quilt top, you will need to cut two border strips for every side that is longer than the width of your fabric. This will require extra yardage. If you prefer unpieced borders, you will need to purchase extra fabric to cut full-length strips from the lengthwise grain.

Borders with Straight-Cut Corners

1. Measure the width of the quilt top through the center. Trim 2 border strips to this measurement, piecing strips as necessary to get the required length. Mark the center of the quilt-top edges and border strips.

2. Pin the border strips to the top and bottom edges of the quilt top, matching center marks and ends and easing as necessary. Stitch in place, then press the seams toward the borders.

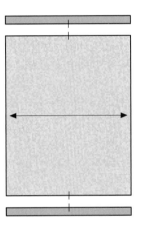

TIP: *If the quilt top is slightly longer than the border, stitch with the quilt top on the bottom. If the reverse is true, stitch with the border on the bottom. The sewing machine's feed dogs will help ease in the extra length.*

3. Measure the length of the quilt top through the center, including the borders just added. Cut border strips to that measurement, piecing strips as necessary. Mark the center of the quilt-top edges and the border strips. Pin the borders to the sides, matching center marks and

ends and easing as necessary. Stitch in place, then press the seams toward the border.

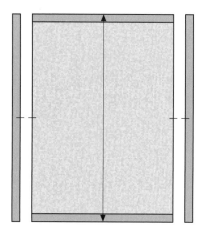

Borders with Corner Squares

1. Measure the width and length of your quilt top through the center. Cut border strips to those measurements, piecing strips as necessary. Mark the center of the quilt top and the border strips. Pin the border strips to the top and bottom edges of the quilt, matching center marks and ends and easing as necessary. Stitch in place, and press the seams toward the border.

2. Sew a corner square to each end of the 2 remaining side borders. Press the seams toward the border strip. Pin the border strips to the sides, matching the center marks and ends and easing as necessary. Stitch in place, and press the seams toward the border.

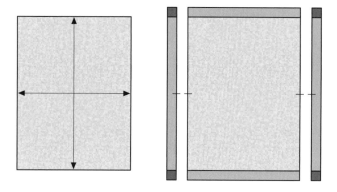

CHOOSING BATTING

To choose a batting for your quilt, you must take into account the quilting method and the quilt's end use. I machine quilt (or have a professional machine quilt) my tops. I usually use cotton batting. Most of today's cotton battings do not require prewashing or the close stitching that older ones did. My batting of choice is Quilter's Dream Cotton, which is available in four weights and six sizes.

I prefer heavyweight batting for bed quilts and wall hangings, and lightweight batting for clothing. Lightweight batting is best for hand quilting.

If you plan to tie your quilt, polyester batting is a good choice. It's also great for children's projects because children seem to prefer the puffy look that polyester provides.

BASTING

1. Press the quilt top from the back—this is the last opportunity to set the seams in the correct direction. Once your seams are set, press from the front. Use spray starch or sizing if desired.

2. Cut the backing and batting about 4" larger than the quilt top on all sides.

3. Press the quilt back. Use spray starch or sizing if desired.

4. Lay the backing, right side down, on a clean, flat surface. Secure it with masking tape (the fabric should be taut but not stretched). Lay the batting on the backing and secure with tape. Add the quilt top, right side up, and secure with tape.

5. Beginning in the center, hand baste horizontally, then vertically in a 4" grid. I prefer hand basting with thread to pin basting because it allows me to machine quilt without stopping to remove pins.

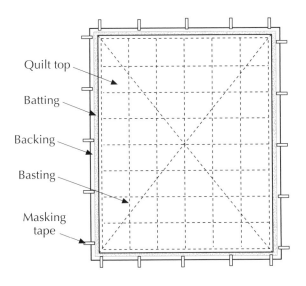

6. After basting the quilt, remove the tape. You are now ready to quilt!

QUILTING

The patterns in this book offer an array of quilting possibilities. Broken Bricks (page 47) is a good pattern for straight-line quilting. Houndstooth (page 9) offers large areas of background in which to stipple or meander quilt. The background bars in Skagit Fields (page 57) are ideal for hand quilting.

I usually machine quilt small projects myself and have larger quilts professionally machine quilted. Sometimes I have only part of a quilt professionally quilted and do the remainder myself. For example, a professional quilted the background triangles in each of my Triangles and Confetti quilts, then I stipple quilted the border. Combining a variety of techniques and threads can be very effective. Professional quilters are a good resource for suggestions on patterns and thread color.

Ultimately, you are the best judge of the quilting that will complement your work. I enjoy designing machine-quilting patterns as I quilt. Working with a vague overall plan, I allow myself freedom and flexibility as I move around the top.

Some excellent quilting books are on the market, and my favorite is *Machine Quilting Made Easy* by Maurine Noble. I recommend that you take a class and practice before attempting your first project.

SQUARING UP A QUILT

When you have completed the quilting, it's time to square up your quilt. This means cutting off the excess backing and batting, as well as cleaning up any threads or uneven sections of border. Use the seam of the outer border as a guide. Align a ruler with the seam and measure to the edge of the quilt in a number of places. Use the narrowest measurement as a guide for positioning your ruler and trimming the excess all around the quilt.

Next, fold the quilt in half, then fold it again in the other direction. Does your quilt have square corners and edges that are equal in length? If not, this is your last chance to correct them. Use a large square ruler to square up the corners.

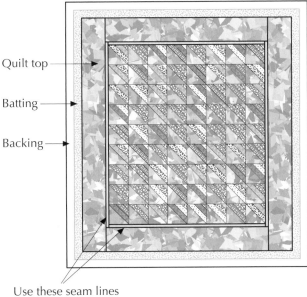

Use these seam lines as a guide for squaring up the quilt.

Use a basting or serpentine stitch around the edge to stabilize the quilt—do not use a zigzag stitch. Once you've squared up your quilt top, you're ready for the finishing touches: the binding, sleeve pocket, and label.

BINDING

The construction of your binding is very important. My work as a judge in quilt competitions has made this clear to me. Participants don't always take care with their bindings, and a poorly made binding can make an otherwise lovely quilt look sloppy. The following binding method combines the best of detail, strength, and beauty.

1. You need enough binding strips to go around the perimeter of the quilt plus 10" for seams and corners. Cut the required number of 3"-wide strips across the width of the fabric. I cut strips on the bias only if I want to take advantage of a plaid print or if I need to fit the binding around rounded corners.

2. Join strips at right angles and stitch across the corner as shown. Trim excess fabric and press the seams open.

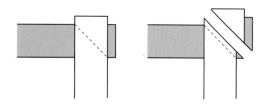

3. Fold the binding in half lengthwise, wrong sides together, and press.

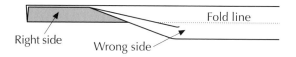

4. Starting 6" from the upper left-hand corner, lay the binding on the quilt top, raw edges even. Begin stitching 4" from the end of the binding (10" from the corner), using a ½"-wide seam allowance.

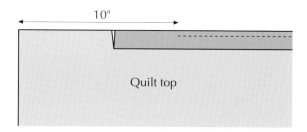

5. Stitch about 2", stop, and cut the threads. Remove the quilt from the machine and fold the binding to the back; it should barely cover the stitching line you just made. If the binding overlaps too much, stitch again, just inside the first stitching line. Not enough to cover the original stitching? Stitch just outside the original stitching. Take out the extra stitches before you proceed.

6. Using the stitching position you determined in step 5, stitch to within ½" of the first corner. Stop, cut the thread, and remove the quilt from the machine.

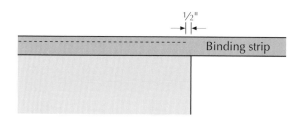

7. Fold the binding as shown to create a mitered corner. Continue stitching to the next corner of the quilt. Repeat the mitering process at each corner.

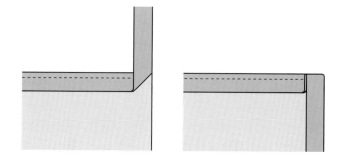

8. After turning the last corner, stitch about 3", then stop. Make sure the 2 ends of the binding overlap at least 4". Cut the threads and remove the quilt from the machine. Measure a 3" overlap and trim the extra binding.

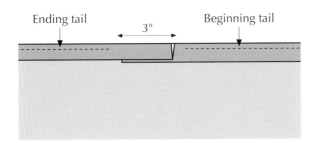

9. Lay the quilt top right side up. Place the unfolded, unstitched tails right sides together at right angles, and pin. Draw a line from the upper left-hand corner to the lower right-hand corner of the binding. Stitch along this line.

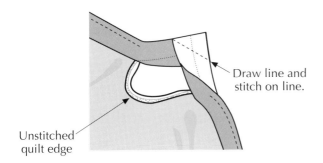

10. Carefully trim the seam allowances to ¼" and press the seam open. Refold the binding in half and press. Finish stitching the binding to the quilt.

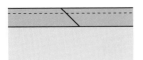

11. Turn the binding to the back of the quilt and pin in place. I pin approximately 12" at a time. Hand stitch the binding to the quilt back, matching the thread to the binding and carefully mitering the corners as you approach them. Hand stitch down each side of the mitered corners.

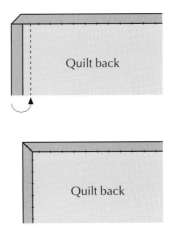

ADDING A SLEEVE

If you want to display your quilt on a wall, you need to add a sleeve to protect your work of art from undue strain.

1. Cut a 7½"-wide strip of backing fabric (if the quilt is wider than 40", you will need to cut 2 strips and stitch them together, end to end). Cut the strip 1" shorter than the width of your quilt. Fold the short ends under ¼", stitch, and press.

2. Fold the sleeve lengthwise, right sides together. Stitch the raw edges together and press. Turn the sleeve right side out and press again.

3. Find the center point of the top edge of the quilt and the center point of the sleeve. Pin the pocket and quilt together, with the folded edge of the sleeve next to the binding. Blindstitch this edge in place.

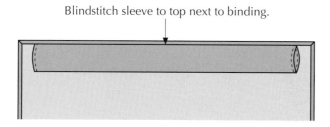
Blindstitch sleeve to top next to binding.

4. Push the bottom edge of the sleeve up just a bit to provide a little give so the hanging rod doesn't put strain on the quilt. Blindstitch the bottom of the sleeve in place. Take care not to catch the front of the quilt as you stitch.

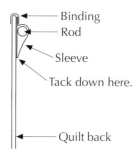
Binding
Rod
Sleeve
Tack down here.
Quilt back

MAKING A LABEL

Labels provide important information about you and your quilt. I make my labels about 4" × 7" so that I have plenty of room. Your labels should include at least the following:

➤ The name of the quilt
➤ Your full name
➤ Your business name, if applicable
➤ Your city, county, province and/or state, and country of residence
➤ The date
➤ Who the quilt was made for if you made it for a specific person, or why you made the quilt if you made it for a particular event

Additional identification is also worth including on a label:

➤ What series the quilt belongs to, if applicable
➤ A quilting teacher's name, if applicable
➤ A story connected with the piece, especially a heartfelt one

There are many ways to make a label. If your sewing machine has a lettering system, use it. If you own or have access to an embroidery machine, use it. Embroidery machines offer wonderful opportunities for embellishing your label. You may even want to create your own logo.

Other label-making methods include drawing and writing with permanent fabric markers, and using photo-transfer techniques. If you use permanent markers, be sure to stabilize the label with freezer paper, Stitch-n-Tear, or interfacing while you letter it.

You may also want to include patches, decals, buttons, ribbons, or lace. Simply stitch them to the label to make it as unique as you are. I also like to include leftover blocks to link the quilt top to the back.

When is the correct time to attach your label? You can sew it to the lower right corner of the quilt back before it is basted or quilted. Or, you can attach your label after the quilting is complete.

About the Author

M'Liss Rae Hawley began her lifelong textile adventure at the age of four by embroidering a pillowcase, and she hasn't stopped since. She took sewing classes in high school, and the nuns discovered quite soon that she had more experience than they did! M'Liss studied at the University of Washington in the Textiles and Clothing department, then continued her studies at Central Washington University's graduate program.

Her many accomplishments include a one-woman quilt show that benefitted Seattle's A Contemporary Theater (ACT), second place in Bernina's first annual national professional competition, first place in Washington's Better Homes & Gardens quilt contest (state level), and dozens of local awards. She also has judged many local and statewide quilt competitions. M'Liss and George (the dachshund) were featured in Bernina of America's Portrait of the Artist ad campaign. M'Liss has even made appearances on PBS cooking and quilting shows.

This is M'Liss's second book with Martingale & Company. Her first was *Mariner's Medallion Using Foundation Paper Piecing*.

M'Liss lives on Whidbey Island, Washington, with her husband, Michael, and their two children, Alexander and  Adrienne. Their small filbert orchard is occupied by four dachshunds, six cats, and an assortment of drop-ins.

NEW AND BESTSELLING TITLES FROM

America's Best-Loved Craft & Hobby Books™

America's Best-Loved Quilt Books®

QUILTING

from That Patchwork Place®, an imprint of Martingale & Company™

Appliqué

Artful Appliqué
Colonial Appliqué
Red and Green: An Appliqué Tradition
Rose Sampler Supreme
Your Family Heritage: Projects in Appliqué

Baby Quilts

Appliqué for Baby
The Quilted Nursery
Quilts for Baby: Easy as ABC
More Quilts for Baby: Easy as ABC
Even More Quilts for Baby: Easy as ABC

Holiday Quilts

Easy and Fun Christmas Quilts
Favorite Christmas Quilts from That Patchwork Place
Paper Piece a Merry Christmas
A Snowman's Family Album Quilt
Welcome to the North Pole

Learning to Quilt

Basic Quiltmaking Techniques for:
  Borders and Bindings
  Curved Piecing
  Divided Circles
  Eight-Pointed Stars
  Hand Appliqué
  Machine Appliqué
  Strip Piecing
The Joy of Quilting
The Quilter's Handbook
Your First Quilt Book (or it should be!)

Paper Piecing

50 Fabulous Paper-Pieced Stars
A Quilter's Ark
Easy Machine Paper Piecing
Needles and Notions
Paper-Pieced Curves
Show Me How to Paper Piece

Rotary Cutting

101 Fabulous Rotary-Cut Quilts
365 Quilt Blocks a Year Perpetual Calendar
Fat Quarter Quilts
Lap Quilting Lives!
Quick Watercolor Quilts
Quilts from Aunt Amy
Spectacular Scraps
Time-Crunch Quilts

Small & Miniature Quilts

Bunnies By The Bay Meets Little Quilts
Celebrate! with Little Quilts
Easy Paper-Pieced Miniatures
Little Quilts All Through the House

CRAFTS
From Martingale & Company

300 Papermaking Recipes
The Art of Handmade Paper and Collage
The Art of Stenciling
Creepy Crafty Halloween
Gorgeous Paper Gifts
Grow Your Own Paper
Stamp with Style
Wedding Ribbonry

KNITTING
From Martingale & Company

Comforts of Home
Fair Isle Sweaters Simplified
Knit It Your Way
Simply Beautiful Sweaters
Two Sticks and a String
The Ultimate Knitter's Guide
Welcome Home: Kaffe Fassett

COLLECTOR'S COMPASS™
From Martingale & Company

20th Century Glass
'50s Decor
Barbie® Doll
Jewelry

Coming to *Collector's Compass* Spring 2001:

20th Century Dinnerware
American Coins
Movie Star Collectibles
'60s Decor